SPLENDOR

SPLENDOR

POEMS BY
STEVE KRONEN

AMERICAN POETS CONTINUUM SERIES, NO. 98

BOA Editions, Ltd. ✳ Rochester, NY ✳ 2006

First Edition
06 07 08 09   7 6 5 4 3 2 1

Publications by BOA Editions, Ltd.—a not-for-profit corporation under section 501 (c)
(3) of the United States Internal Revenue Code—are made possible with the assistance of
grants from the Literature Program of the New York State Council on the Arts;
the Literature Program of the National Endowment for the Arts; County of Monroe, NY;
the Lannan Foundation for support of the Lannan Translation Selection Series;
Sonia Raiziss Giop Charitable Foundation; Mary S. Mulligan Charitable Trust;
Rochester Area Community Foundation; Arts & Cultural Council for Greater Rochester;
Steeple-Jack Fund; Elizabeth F. Cheney Foundation; Eastman Kodak Company;
Chesonis Family Foundation; Ames-Amzalak Memorial Trust in memory of Henry Ames,
Semon Amzalak and Dan Amzalak; and contributions from many individuals nationwide.

See Colophon on page 80 for special individual acknowledgments.

Cover Design: Steve Smock
Cover Art: "Crystal" by Robert Marx, courtesy of the artist
Interior Design and Composition: Richard Foerster
Manufacturing: McNaughton & Gunn, Lithographers
BOA Logo: Mirko

Library of Congress Cataloging-in-Publication Data

Kronen, Steve.
  Splendor / by Steve Kronen.— 1st ed.
     p. cm. — (American poets continuum series, v. 98)
  ISBN 1–929918–78–X (pbk. : alk. paper)
  I. Title. II. Series.

PS3561.R585S65 2006
811'.54—dc22

2005033986

NATIONAL
ENDOWMENT
FOR THE ARTS

BOA Editions, Ltd.
Thom Ward, Editor
David Oliveiri, Chair
A. Poulin, Jr., President & Founder (1938–1996)
260 East Avenue, Rochester, NY 14604
www.boaeditions.org

State of the Arts

NYSCA

for my father, Phil
1928–1995

and for my daughter, Sophie

Contents

SPLENDOR

The Wide World

Moses in the bulrushes, lost, the clouds
a whirligig above him. The entire
world so far, its gyre
unbearable, sickens him, and a small crowd
peers down gawking when he comes to rest
wedged in the weeds somewhere far from home
and is cradled lovingly in the arm
of a daughter of a despot dressed
in bracelets that make a familiar sort of music
to a baby. Like the memory
of a memory in an adult,
who remembers bells, and a cobalt
sky, and that the air was summery,
and that all of it would change before he grew used to it.

Mint of the Empire

What strange animal sleeps
curled around my father's
heart tonight? Moon silvers
his eyes, mint
of the empire. Father,
I'd say when he was
alive, explain this vain,
wild country, bristling
and quilled, and mighty
and loud. Land of Shaky Heart, of
the tall night-windows rattling,
and of the tired, dumb beast, teeth bared
a little, wrapped fast about its luscious fruit.

Signs and Portents

If the directions say, *Dip the baby*, then
dip the baby, submerge even the heel.
Victory is assured? Whose?
Please ask whose. The gods are clever
and we are vain and misread
even the obvious. Even the simple world
which warns us and warns us.
Best kill no one, even if they bear
no paternal resemblance, even if they are rude
and obstructive. Disregard
the bicameral mind and all its fond
ambiguities. And should the heart,
which hasn't the luxury
of ambiguity, come from the front
with its keen directive, please take heed
this once, *All hangs in the balance*,
says the hurried scrawl,
you cannot give too much.

Dreaming of Mexico, Ambrose Bierce, and Weldon Kees

You won't find a new country, won't find another shore.
This city will always pursue you.
                                        —Cavafy

Like a few good yeggs must after a theft,
shoulder their goods refusing to halt
and never gaze backwards lest they be salted
away for years, they had their fill and left.

As even the most lawful are tempted.
The broker whose boredom is violence
to his heart flees with paints to the South Sea Islands
where girls have good skin and he is prompted

to capture the fierce pastel beauty
of their heliotropic faces. Or Job,
the blithe, unwitting subject of a probe
about the nature of faith and duty

must—considering the boils and doubt
delivered from, of all quarters, heaven
and Him he trusted most—be forgiven
if once or twice he thought of getting out.

What drives a quiet man to up and go,
leaving behind a puzzled kith
and kin, making for hinterlands, if not Death's,
the interiors of a golden Mexico

or some vague Mexico of the mind?
There we'll find them, our heads deep in pillows
approaching sleep's border and their hellos—
two silhouettes urging us to unwind

with umbrellaed drinks and join them in a swim.
How content we are here, brown and sturdy,
having commended the exhausted body
to X out with each spread-eagled limb

the toiling world beyond—every chest-crushing
burden thrown off: the long lines of dead
relatives, the long sweated deadlines, red-
figured checkbooks, the brow-brushing

wing of our own impending end—over
and done! free to mount our Rocinante
(if not our own tired ass) and go. Or Dante-
like, climb up and out to the star-covered

sky, only to find a universe undomed,
lacking distal point and center. *What region
is this? What landmarks? What terrified pigeon
flaps wildly approaching or leaving home?*

Autobiography: The Early Years

"Bring out your dead!" and I did, roadside
service; Auntie Mame and Uncle Joe (and Little Timmy)
                                        hauled away—
my childhood stacked like cordwood
on the rickety cart with the huge
wooden wheels half sunk in the muddy lane,
but turning still, round and round.

And spring once more, the sun made its rounds
over the mountainside
above our drafty house where the weak had lain
all season. How they weighed
upon me, their presence huge
in the small room of thatch and wood

and shuttered windows which would
not keep out the wind or the rounds
sung over the sour beer in the huge
outdoors beyond our door. Mame, lying there, sighed
just to hear their harmonizing way
down the treeless lane.

Oh I was sad seeing where the three had lain
pitching back and forth all winter on their slatted, wooden
beds, but figured there was no way
I, a small boy with small hands, could bring them round,
though I rubbed Mame's feet once, turned Timmy on his side.
Their intransigence was huge

and I busied myself before the huge
blue light of the television, the laying
of my small hands upon it brightening my side
of the room where I sat each morning, wooed

by the shimmer of the round
test pattern and the farm report all the way

from Clover City. But that light convinced me of a better way
and during commercials I wrapped Mame's huge
shawl, the one from Paris she said, around
her skinny body as I kept an ear cocked to the lane,
placed the flap of his hat over Joe's wooden
gaze, and tucked Timmy's arms to his side,

glancing sidelong from screen to lane
where the cart would come our way and those voices
call us to the huge world still turning round and round.

Song of Vegetable Love

I on my fenceside, you in your leafy aisle let

your bright hose open like the islet
of Langerhans at Thanksgiving time,

watering your fennel, and your licorice, your thyme
and dill, trilling up and down the rows,

something something a red, red rose,
and my heart's magnet and poles

all spin and pull, the very pulls
that of course make up the whole

of love and you in each little hole
poking your fingers and the incandescent green

feathery stalks that sun and water agreeing
should not from this earth perish, should

do the helpful thing, rain gentle as a parachute.

The World's Deserts

on the occasion of our wedding

How long it must have taken; the Magi
lumbering to Baby Jesus swaddled
in the buoyant light and his parents'

last tattered blanket, the brittle
night air chafing as they navigated
the insistent stars. Or the Mormons

trudging past saguaros pointing
to the unbearable sky
whence their directions came

as the pearl-small sun hung shadows
between their blistered feet. The tongues
of their oxen would not have moistened

a postage stamp for a card
to the parsley-green hills
back home, away from where the heart

is made more arid daily. It's always
this hard going, boots mired
in the dream-heavy substance

of the too-real world, praying
that this time, over the next rise. . . .
Yet, who will understand, years from now,

when the Gobi, the Sahara,
even Death Valley, are only names
for prefab retirement homes

risen on the shores
of Lake Mojave? And which tenant there
will explain the Israelites'

40-year meander, a conga line
of marathon dancers dreaming of Canaan,
washing down their withered bread

with the promise of milk and honey?
Even the unstinting Antarctic—
whiter than the Word before it was spoken,

a land where fingers, toes, then finally
limbs are made insensate
and a man is no more than a seething stump,

a plexus of unmeetable desires
and memories of childhood when curtains
flapped beside his autumn bed

and the first star rose in the sky
to sing him to sleep. And there,
other stars, more it's said

than all the sands on all the beaches,
kaleidoscoped before him as they do now
forming pictures before us in this cool night

a horse with wings, and there—
a barking dog, and there—a skinny man
holding fast to a beautiful woman

having come many hard miles to find each other.

River

for Ivonne, and for her mother, Mercedes Fernandez,
dead of cancer, 1965

The lights along the river were dim.
A long river, they shone
as from a dream; white bone-
like lights the two of you watched shimmer

in the water and air, unable to reckon
which reflected which. She took
your hand and placed it on her chest like a book
set face down for a second

so she might absorb just what she'd read.
And your hand fit between her breasts where the ribs curl
slowly up and away like the hull
of your boat, which was silent but for what you heard

through your hand: the pull and drift the heart keeps.
You'd curl yourself into that prow and sleep
if allowed, so that nothing could dislodge

you, though you fear, though you always fear,
the berth's too thin to bear
your weight and she'll begin, as you know she must, her passage.

Sparrow Falling

The barn ablaze atop the hill brighter
         than the moon, and the cows, no longer stupid,
                  terrified, lowing, their big eyes,
which the children love to draw with crayons,
         turning colors in the disturbed light.
                  One accident too many? cigarette tossed aside
like a hurt prematurely from the heart? or
         spontaneous combustion—scoffed at
                  in the tables of actuaries
until it happens to a neighbor
         of a neighbor of a neighbor—a pile
                  of oily rags and the barometer
rising. Or merely lightning and thunder—hot air
         meets cold, a terrible vacuum ensues and
                  kaboom! Like hard voices from the next room
or the rumble of ice floes
         in our children's dreams as the moon bears
                  down on the house like the eye
that watches us constantly, all of us asleep in our beds
         —the sparrow
                  falling—and that guides, almost always,
our every step.

This Kingdom

for my father

The seed, the pith, the stone,
the marrow in the bone,
pillow we rest our head upon,

the appropriate passage fallen open in the text
that will or will not instruct.
Assuming gravity, drawing one object to the next

and depending at last on nothing but mercy,
this world that makes us dizzy
spins and spins yet stirs

the breeze that soothes the fever.
You're tired, Father, lie down; how severe
this chastisement of mass—bag of silver

chinging in our pockets—a fulcrum
shifting that no longer bears the kingdom
to which we've come.

And kingdom—a habit inbred;
gospel of heart and kernel and germ fast spread,
the hundred thousand miles between the pillow and your head.

With Child

TV and book covers lousy with angels
and you growing fatter daily, hungry
with a steam shovel's hunger, ointments and gels
smeared across your stretched skin and dumbly

she grows. *World*, cries Edgar, *O World!*
and there's no getting around it, unwieldy
it's too big to bear, will make the soul curdle
in its paper shell, will make it worldly

and crush the heart as surely as strips
of spring grass are pulled up by a bull
and ground between its bicuspids. The lips
grow green with the delicious drool

as he grinds beneath his hooves the sloppy cud.
Know that it won't stop for her, made from our blood.
Yet, tell her to come, the air thickens
with angels. Come. Hurry and quicken.

In the Hangar of Brisbee, Oklahoma, 1933

Sleepy, my father liked to lie on its floor and stare
through the August heat at the quivering air gathered above

as if it were the dome of heaven and he lay
at the top of the beneficent world dreaming of flight

—all of them together once more—Mom, Pop, and son
packed like bonbons into their seats, white scarves

flapping like birthday ribbons. How he'd pray, he told me,
that the pilot would take them up where the thin wind

makes the eyes tear and carry them across the farm
where his parents were raised—two bucktoothed cousins

hauling sorghum from the wagon to the barn. And there
they'd see the farmhouse and the chalky soil, sky rippling

like the northern lights over the quilt that unraveled
beyond the gray roofs of Brisbee and Clover City.

How they'd marvel at themselves, a family in flight,
and at their shadow, no larger it seemed, than the decimal point

that brought the loan officer to their porch, than the pupil
still swimming in his milky eye.

The Hippopotamus at the Zoological Gardens, Regent's Park, 1852

after the photograph by Juan de Borbon

The eight gray visitors behind him, long dead, even
the youngest—a boy in a cap and starched collar
warning us with his eyes—lean

for support on the horizontal bar
behind the cage. Together they weigh less
than the satisfied brute, asleep

and dreaming before the pool
that reflects, upside down, his great
dreamlike mass. He is

the center of the universe.
How to explain this irrefutable
encroachment of the other world? How

come to terms with his great Buddha heart?
By now the grand industries of Birmingham
and Oldham have blackened the skies and good Pip

is making his way in London, is halfway up
the swaying ladder to a classless and godless
heaven. Darwin organizes his notes and omens

are everywhere. Yet love, too
is possible and draws them, strangers all, to wonder
at the awful embodiment of their own

Stygian sloth sprawled there upon the cool bricks
where he, hours before, lowered himself. Surely,
the boy is convinced, something can wake him,

raise the animal to all fours to lumber forth
and block out the sun, touch them with the hem
of his big black shadow, a mountain that comes to them

and under which they can sleep, a solar eclipse
that passes slowly, and resets, starting now,
the ticking clocks of their white astonished faces.

The Coroner's Report

Behind the ribs, Miss Havisham's heart,
despite its human wish, remembered:
mitral valve opened and mitral valve shut,

blood pumped through its one-way shunt
and like Miss Havisham in her chambers,
wended through the beating heart.

Bend a stethoscope to where she hurt,
(peel the wedding gown yellowed to tinder,)
and you'd hear the mitral valve open and shut.

(It's not unlike the familiar stutter
one's own heart makes, the lurch, the stumble.)
The racket inside Miss Havisham's heart,

had ear been placed to chest, would exhort
us listen to the timbre
of the mitral valve opening, shutting,

banging through the night like a shutter
in the rain, rattling like a dormer
in the very house you live in. The heart
opened like a flower. Unremarkable, her case was shut.

The Poet at Seven

for Donald Justice

A crescent moon above the house, then gone.
He'd rise for school, some oatmeal then a sweater
the color of the yard, and swing his lunchbox,
—the dead-weight thermos overhead, the center
of gravity lurching from his heart to navel.
And breath would feather from his nose and mouth,
appear and disappear like silky scarves
pulled end to end from a magician's sleeve.
He'd follow, a small god behind a small cloud,
and watch a hundred birds suddenly swivel
on the sky, turn as one as though surrendered
to some voice he strained to hear but couldn't coax
from the air, nor decipher the black letters
they spelled along the wire as they stared down.

Mapless World

for Ivonne

> *. . . Noah opened the window. . . . And he sent forth*
> *a raven . . .*
>
> —Genesis 8:6–7

The clouds and sky as close as sea and coral,
He had no home or bearings left, and hurled
Out toward the newfound sun a raven
That it return with sprigs of some green haven
And fix a point upon the mapless world.

And still, the gyroscope heart blurs as it whirls,
Righting itself between the earth and heaven
And drags with it the axis of its circle
Till the center of the universe is plural
And no direction clear.
⠀⠀⠀⠀⠀⠀⠀⠀⠀⠀⠀All night some feral
Creature strops claws upon the air and snarls
In its sleep. Stormheads gather and are riven.
And I, who leave my door at my own peril,
Sleep beside you now, and have no fear of moving.
You whose steady breath all night unfurls
Like a flag above a land richly believed in,
Who leaves the window wide to let the dove in.

One Wind

for my father

Heart's red fountain; can it soak
the dun acres? North,
an arid wind;
and what does it intend?
Cover, cover the earth,
tangle the hair he stroked.

Bright fountain; can it soak
the bitter soil? West,
an arid wind;
and what does it intend?
Undo the few things blessed,
unhang his scarf and cloak.

Red fountain, saturate
the sandy plain. An arid wind
made the weathervane grate,
blew to the East
and has not ceased,
blew hard and made him bend.

I heard him choke
in a brittle field where a south
and arid wind
still blows as it intends.
It parched his puzzled mouth,
blew far his risen smoke,

blows far and never ends.

London, 1940

The heat came on as did the radio
      —*Eine Kleine Nachtmusik*—and the room
    was suddenly a dull man's idea
of heaven, radiator steam
       softening the corners of the ceiling,
         the windows snow-stricken. Half asleep in that cloud
we lay on the sofa, each feeling
    the breath of the other on our necks, and not loud,
   the music was only the thought of
             music—insidious, soothing, omnipresent—
like our school days' conception of God's love
    which for our good was unrelenting
  and could have found us anywhere. Even in the tunnels,
       waiting, the low note of engines above the Channel.

Pantoum: Polish Farmhouse, 4 AM, 1943

All night the long whistle and bell
barely made out through the rain
are nearly unintelligible
in the procession of the train.

The cars sound through the wind and rain
and though we count we lose their number.
The endless procession of the train
comes over our house like a kind of slumber.

We count the cars but lose their number.
Too many we tell ourselves yet listen
just the same for some kinder slumber
to fall upon our house. They've come a distance

and though we need sleep we listen
for voices the passing cars conjure.
They've come a great distance
and their sounds endure

for they do not stop and their passing conjures
something almost intelligible,
something we didn't listen for, but endures,
like a whistle or the final note of a bell.

Marianne Moore Late at Night

The last great light before dark and then everything
dark but the windows of the tallest offices

and the face of the clock on the tallest
building, its hands watched long enough,

still moving. In one dim square, someone
worries the yellow light, casting shadows,

or is a shadow—it's Marianne Moore!
everyone home but her, rifling the drawers

of the rich executives as she studies
receipts and memos, a letter in draft

in which someone is explaining something
difficult, telling a lie that's almost obviously

a lie. This treachery, it breaks her heart; how
the world keeps turning even as the carbon stains

the fingers of Miss Moore who will smudge
her mother's cheek hours later after flying home

across the East River, over the empty Brooklyn avenues
where the milkman squints at the fine script of the note

and the empties jostle in his hand. He peers
in to where she should lie sleeping,

sheets rising atop the breasts flattened
across her chest. How he would, if Miss Moore'd

allow it, peel his muddy shoes away
and slide quietly in beside her,

one hand light upon a nipple and
a cold dew-heavy bottle against her brow,

whispering the words he'd written for her,
explaining planets and Guernseys and atoms

until her breath blooms apple-sweet above her parted mouth
and the sun, once more, outlines the bird-bright eaves.

Hallaballoo

Chin to sky, Mr. Rictus is tracking a cumulus
which wanders, he says, lowly as a cloud.
The ample sky is humming—an airplane gone
from sight—and all of Saturday is green and blue.
Consider, says Mr. Rictus, *the ignorant Armenians*
who clash by night and not one doubloon
from the jewel-encrusted chests of their mullahs,
not a word from their fan-cooled pashas
is weighted with sufficient clout
to make for a moment the bellicose minions
sheath their falchions or their passions.
But none of this compares, he says, *with the hallaballoo*
raging inside the human viscera. When Maud Gonne
returned his ring, Keats's each enfeebled lung
burst open, he who'd tried to save Dublin
with his pen. But Keats, he says, *was short and life is long.*
All of which seems suspect and I'm thinking, No sir, a
bit fishy this. Except maybe the love and human viscera.

The Comforts of Middle Age

*Every path but your own is the path of fate. Keep on your
own path, then.*
—*Walden*

*One's own dharma, though imperfect, is better than the
dharma of another well discharged.*
—*Bhagavad Gita 3:35*

Day's last light and stars above this train
and the preening, off-key violins of brakes
rise in indignation to the strain

placed on them at each stop. The floor shakes
and the ground, nauseating and blurry
beyond our windows, coalesces, takes

its proper form. Thoreau, who loved the fury
and rough majesty of the train which *snorts
like thunder shaking the earth with its feet*, the flurry

of *silver and golden wreaths* from the gushed retorts
of its furnace, said trains set the nation's clocks,
and we live, he added, *the steadier for it.*

Steadiness, a longed-for pillow after an awkward
day, an awkward life, plumped and cool
beneath my head. Steadiness in the walk

he took daily by his American pool
of good sense and calm, up the rise, across
the pike to Concord, past smiths, and school-

yard, and shops to a home-cooked meal, wind-tossed
wilds behind him. And how should we begrudge
him, our deliberate-living naturalist,

these few small comforts, who, by evening, trudged
back toward his tiny cabin and listened
beside the water on the forest's edge,

to trains at night, ghostly and insistent,
approach from somewhere far away, leave
for somewhere far away, engineer listing

through a window to eye the tracks that weave
themselves across his Massachusetts hills,
counting the stops until his head, if briefly,

will lean, as to a loved one, on a pillow.

Brief Monologue of the Mirror

Dear one, I will deny the distance between
us, I, who have nothing to give but myself.
Once, peering beyond the glazy surface,
you murmured as before an altar.

How imperceptibly the light has altered.
Yet, I'll meet, halfway, as always, your face
and proffer, respectfully, my salver.
I will not flinch, my own, my nearly loved twin.

Flowers, Things Vital and Unvital

after Akhmatova

Smells of flowers, things vital and unvital,
fill the hallways, sweep the opened rooms.
In the garden, piles of vegetables
spill back onto the shoveled loam,

and despite this last March wind
the tarps are lifted, furled buds
are transferred pot to bed. The pond
is rippled with a colored mud:

a blanket stitched with patterns.
A shaking boy, hands stretched wide,
says, *On the bottom, bright as lanterns*
a gold carp lives with his gold carp bride . . .

A Road in Agrigentum

after Quasimodo

The wind that set the horses' manes
to fire angling across the plains,
bleaches this sandstone, wears down
the hearts of these statues tumbled to the ground.
And an old hurt drains the older soul,
returns now with the wind to roil
delicate scents from this green, green moss
which covers at last the bewildered eyes
of all these giants so suddenly driven
over the treacherous lip of heaven.

But, deeper your ache when toward the boats,
anchored like morning stars, the notes
of the wagoner drone in the little time
left you. Jew's-harp moaning, he'll climb
the moon-blanched hill beside the groves
of the nearly-hushed Saracen olives.

Homesickness

after Du Bellay

Fortunate the man who, chastened
by the foreign, sails back to his harbor
and spies, past mast and spire and neighbor's
chimney smoke, his own home and, like Jason
or Ulysses, returns to stay. What season
will set me in my yard to wander the arbor
of that house whose green port and starboard
are all the ocean I need gaze on?

Richer the simple house of wattled walls
and ungabled roof where my father had lain
and his father, than all the marbled halls
of the Parisian gentry who crowd the Seine
with their craft, and whose white faces would seem
insubstantial as clouds above my Anjou stream.

The Neglected Moon

after Baudelaire

Moon, our mothers and fathers gaped
at you, their eyes full of you parading
up the blue-black sky, stars and planets draped
behind. And now, illuminating

our triumphant back rooms, we sleep (small planets
ourselves), tired from love, slack-jawed, our teeth
gleaming and white like you. Shine on your poets
stymied at their papers, and snakes that writhe

in open fields, full of desire. But to shine
on that handsome boy who refuses to age
and sleeps till noon . . . well . . . and you, tracing lines

round your eyes before the mirror, yellow frock
disheveled, rubbing just a little rouge
on nipples he wouldn't fondle or suck. . . .

The Last Evening

after Rilke

And night and the large wheels turning,
rutting the earth toward the cannon's thunder.
He looked up from the piano to find her
across the room, her face a warning
and a prayer, mirroring, he realized, his own.
Outside, a fresh wind ruffled the trees above
the house and she grew more seductive
in his gaze as he continued with the song.

Then suddenly, both faces dulled.
And he stopped playing while she listened
to the wind and to her heart. His field cap
on the table now seemed strangely distant,
folded neatly as though it were an ancient map
holding within itself all the monstrous world.

Digging

All day a gauze of rain.
His big body'd given way
and the stolid, hulking bones

turned to lace. Transverse
section fine as a doily,
the doctor told the interns

after he'd signed the certificate.
Moon powder, his wife said
after the ceremony, turning

the urn upside down and shaking it
like a stubborn jar in the kitchen
after midnights, the two of them

naked and squinting in the icebox door.
Back in bed he'd slept like a bear
except for the fretwork going on

inside the bones, steady
tunneling like the subways beneath
their building—hewed underground

early in the century with the heave
and ho and sweat of men.
But before the end, in their bed,

she could hear the scratch and thwack
working its way through him night
and day, until it had become background,

a rumble of subway
up through the feet, the constant undersound
below his breath that kept her up nights

beside him who slept. Pay it no mind,
he'd tell her in the morning,
he who loved her and seemed to come back,

slower each time,
all the way from China
just to tell her.

Beholden: On the Birth of My Daughter

On the eye's own screen
the shining world's disturbed, turned
upside down and seen

only in the burned-
out, ashy degrees of black
and white that the mourned

exact, till sent back
from the brain and set aright.
The drear bric-a-brac

of this life's made bright
there, shapes we're grateful for traced
in the mind's own light

as when all earth's grays
were turned by Ceres to green.
So we come to grace—

the weighted fruit gleaned
and eaten, the beam removed
and the mote pulled clean—

all for those shapes love
takes: your face before my face.

Arguing About Moving to a Larger Home—What I Should Have Said

Giving no quarter,
you and I
might live beneath a cloud-drenched sky,

though, back to back,
agreeing, share it,
find we wake inside a garret,

with walls aslant,
yet floorboards level,
we'll bank what fires keep our hovel

and ear to chest
hear how a heart's meant
to echo through a small apartment

where living cramped,
yet living close,
we're apt to amble through a house,

its portals wide,
the heart's expansion
sets the boundaries of a mansion,

each broad arcade
awash with solace
of fountains in a summer palace

and gazing past the walls we live in,
dwell beneath no sky
but heaven.

After the Argument

Through the window by the bookcase,
His bobbing hat above the bouquets.

Eugene Debs in Heaven

Forced from the world, I'd have stayed forever
and worked the train yards of Terre Haute.
Lay down your tools when the workweek's over.

To feed our families we curried favor
from careful men; we listened to the engines hoot
their pent-up force into the world. Staid, forever

making do, when Pullman paid no wage to cover
our ice in summer, in winter, heat,
we dropped our tools before the week was over

and stopped his trains. Brash with the fervor
of hungry men, we pilfered food and heart-
sized coals forced from the world. I'd have stayed forever,

spinning Earth off a shovel's lever
—Earth spins and toils though its workers halt—
and laid down my tools when the week was over.

Released from prison, all spring I shivered,
all that autumn sick with sweat. I did not hate.
Forced from the world, I'd have stayed forever;
lay down your tools when the workweek's over.

Rocking Chairs from the Thirties

Under a mocking wind, you'll throw yourselves,
dolorous and shamed Rockettes of the porch,
into the old routine. And a little chilly, repeat, again—
two, three, four—your confused and nearly remembered
drills. Should you kick high, something
might give, who once welcomed flesh upon

your flesh, and gave what you got, sweaty
on a summer's night when the breezes
were somewhere in the low pasture. And relished,
even when young, the timid cadences
of the old themselves, who also creaked
and have, for a long time now, not been seen.

On Turning Fifty

for Larry Apple on his birthday

It is not the spirit now, but the arch
of each foot that must be buttressed; to lift
is no shame to the lifter; neither church
nor state can refuse the determined drift
back toward the earth. Yet not with the lurch
of the frightened driver learning to shift
for the first time, death-grip on the clutch
as he gropes from forty into fifty.

But gently now, the way a sheet is spread
fresh from the line above the unmade bed
falling so slowly it hovers midspace
and seems angels lie round a picnic cloth.
The harried driver thinks such ease is sloth;
the sated angels know it's only grace.

His Penis at Eighty

Sing Muse, of the last-picked for the home team. Dawdler.
Drooler. Stretched out past the 7th inning.
My muffled cowbell now the cows have maundered
back into the corn. My mumbler, scanning
his ground with the hunched, kyphotic shoulders
of an asthmatic squinting at a penny.
Who, with knowing smile, recited Baudelaire
to the girls' French club and now, past cunning,
would lecture on the necessity of candor.
Yet one time thought a kiss, heart humming
like a hive, might bring order to his disordered
seasons and right the tilting globe spinning
about its pole. Sing of my wounded soldier
without his purple heart on. And the frightened whinny

of the unlapped horse watching others pass it.
As once, above, we watched the North Star fading,
diluted with morning—for it had grown early
having grown late. Sing of growing late.
Of my lost compass. Of my dissolute, my desolate,
my one, my only, my sad-faced basset.
Raise, if just a voice, a chorus of *Tom Dooley*,
and of how we watched that star, pulsing, wish-laden.

Our Home Movies

*"There, there, all of this is only a movie, young man, only
a movie," but I look up once more at the terrifying sun . . .*
—Delmore Schwartz, "In Dreams
Begin Responsibilities"

We watched them in the living room
and counted candles for the cake,
kitchen clock looming
over the oven to make
childhood inch forward more slowly.
This is pre-Beatles,
pre-Stones, fish is holy
enough to render our lunchrooms meatless
on Fridays. Pre-Dallas. Pre-November.
Yet even now, years from home,
whenever I've watched what Zapruder filmed
that day, I think of Delmore Schwartz—his parents
on the screen—rising to shout, overwhelmed
and half sick as he remembers
just what's going to happen. Nothing warrants
what's going to happen:

One by one the frames are dropping,
and each moment, unbound
from its little cage, makes the light stammer
and the Texas sun dazzles the chrome
of their blue-black car which rounds
that corner again. Nothing will stop them, keep
the hands from flying up
elbows wide to the throat or
the head from lurching
back as she clambers
to the trunk reaching
for something unreachable.   And when, motor

still running, the footage
slips its spool, we protect our
eyes in that too-bright room. The projector
above us and its played-out ribbon
whites out the screen where the car has driven,
imperious as a sun returned to mark our age.

Perma-War

They'll burn my crops and hoard my oil
though I've broken their intricate code
and hold in my hands the very cables

they pass in the night from cell to cabal—
little rat-faced men in coteries
who'd hoard my crops and burn my oil.

I've seen it all before, the royal
family in cellars like lambs in a cote.
Had they the chance, they'd cut my cables

and then my neck, agents from Kabul
in pearly turbans, from Moscow in coats
who'd burn my hordes and crop my oil.

Why won't they love me? Their hot hearts roil
at mention of mine. Their eyes are cold.
My cart's piled high on a cobble-

stone street, light from my city a cannibal
fire, its smoke an inelegant coda.
For they'd burn my crops and hoard my oil.
They'd hold like reins my very cables.

Cleave

My daughter fighting sleep surrenders
at last the heft of her head to my shoulder

and leans, corporeal now and weighty,
against my body the mass of her body

who, smaller than a missed period
at sentence end, multiplied to the myriad

(the atom cloven to produce a blast
to shake the earth cleaves to make a blast-

ocyst), accruing cell to self, as must a pearl,
making organs, a child, a world,

a multitude, a speck,
this breath, for now, upon my neck

Baby Daughter Half Asleep in a Swing

The world and what she makes of it sprawls
before her—a rollicking sky and earth.
Weightless a moment, her arms and haunches
thicken with centrifuge. Back and forth
she goes, the blanched November sun lulls
her to a stupor. Such light should keep her conscious

who churned from the womb wide-eyed (though coated
with a Lethe ooze as if to forget
the blurry sway of the world she'd chosen
and pass from her mother without regret).
Galileo once clocked, by beats encoded
in his wrist, a censer's swing. Mass and motion

measured time. Worlds in his telescopes
pulled on each other: starry valences
of moons and planets wandering through space,
all tethered by delicate balances
at the far-swung ends of their unseen ropes.
I know time and motion will wear in her face:

Wallendas, the Hanged Man, the sagging Christ,
Harold Lloyd dangling from a city clock,
Jonathan Edwards' tenuous spider
scribbling damnation in its fiery arc.
All of it, even now, pounds in her wrist,
the green world falling away from under.

Canzone: Deed and Grace

for Anthony Hecht

And nearly there, we were wondering again,
how will we, dusty from travel, know
the wheat from chaff, casting about again,
plodding too far into the woods to again
find our way back. Whether by deed or grace
or, if need be, subterfuge—how regain
what we frittered away on our way. Or again,
coin weighted on the palm, fingers unbound,
barter and continue where we were bound.
Toward the city, gleaming with its gainly,
handsome skyscrapers and below-the-surface
trains rumbling the concrete up to the surface,

unloading like picked fruit from a basket their surfeits
of tumbled workers. Hope then for some gain,
perform as you must, smooth like a sheet the surface
of your life, confronting mornings a half-sure face
in the bathroom mirror. No use giving notice,
vacating your tipsy life. You'll surface
daily, sky through the grate a lakey surface,
climb the subway steps with the casual grace
that accrues from repeated motion, and perhaps grace
a little with the color of eye and cheek, the surface
world—a Persephone taking in air, unbound
awhile, eyes dilating to make out the boundaries

of buildings or, somewhere beyond, cows and lake. They're bound
together by your eye. Once, on the surface
of the lake, a breeze inscribed its glyphs which were bound
to explain, if read rightly, to ungag you, unbind
you from an old, inconsequential bargain.

(Made, it seems, with a younger self who was bound
by it, hewed to it through the years when bounty
seemed as close as unpicked fruit, through know-
nothing, then seasoned years—sealed without knowing
why). Bargain's still working—an Old Faithful unbound
from below—unchanging as those cows grazing
mornings, called from the lake under the grays

of evening where a last ochre sun graces
picnickers by the lake. Food boundless.
Butter sweet. Laughter. And the coup de grace?
It could have been you. Honeyed Earl Greys
in hand, steam rising from each surface.
And the tea leaves? Your royal birth, some Greystoke
left to fend, alone in a graceless
faraway hut, the chittering, gainsaying
dark swelling outside once again
and a Jacob's ladder of vines gracing
the limbs beyond the door. How to know?:
Grasp one in your hands and express your noble

character so long hidden? Or stick with the notion
of laying low, muted light grazing
your roof at dusk, a fine golden gnosis
seeping through the fronds etching its notations
around you? Either will do, bound
as we are to choose our own forced card. Look, nothing
up the sleeve. In the unrolled hand nothing
but the coin found behind an ear, one surface
stamped with bird or building, the other surface
bright with its little glyphs. Yet, how to know
its exchange when the gold standard shifts again
with revived reports of El Niño, again

with the width of this year's tie? The ties that have bound
are working still. And yet how bright the surface
of the apple on its branch. Reach. The notes

of birds. The cows' eyes. The sun, its graceful
light obscuring the coin you've flipped again.

The World Before Them

Actually, it was sweet and heavy with juice
and we passed it back and forth, a river
of nectar running down her chin and mine
until we were full and our faces shone
and could not tell receiver from giver.
I loved its weight in my hand, bruised
just a little from having fallen
from those high, green limbs. And we took its seed
and planted more when we left that place
so we'd always be sure to have its taste
upon our tongues. That was her idea, freed
us from worrying about the future. And all in
all, we didn't. We ate them to the core.
It's as though we'd been provided for.

Splendor

Old Mr. Rictus beside the yew shrub, moon
coming up behind him like a halo,
though I'm not buying any of it. *Halooo,*
he says, long, a Holstein mooing.
Out for your evening constitutional? Smiles.
Yes, to air is bovine. I've come some miles
myself. Come some miles to find myself here
now, before your small self to suffer,
as they say, the little Chileans. I raise
an eyebrow and turn to home. The moon's rays
bathe the street in a kind of splendor
and walking under the arching, shining leaves
I'm, for a moment, in spite of him, relieved
of the weight inside my chest, of its terrible and/or.

A Boy and His Dog

And up and down the ragged coast
gulls draft on the high blue airs, coast
the underside of a nimbus
drifting past reach, big as a bus
on a high and skinny road. Wave
good-bye. It is leaving now. Waive
any right to see it again.
The bright stars, the prickly stars, gain
on the sky. They sprawl forever,
and you'll not, with all your effort,
see an end to them, never see
where the sky goes—you think, *Mercy,*
have mercy. The cloud, out of sight,
has floated now to some far site
on the other side of the world,
has changed shapes so many times, whirled
about, you'd never recognize
it, even if you kept your eyes
fixed up beyond the dark that spans
the night, the entire expanse
of it. Yet watch for its return,
stay steady, it'll come back, turn
some corner. If you threw your heart
upward into the dark, threw hard,
you'd never hear it hit bottom,
some small echo come back. But I'm
patient, you think, can wait; either
a slight ripple through the ether
will tickle my skin, or my ear
will tingle inside and I'll hear
it, my heart, come as through a sea,
come from far away; *have mercy,*
it might say, great shaggy being

trying to grasp just where it's been,
where it's going, fully explain,
calmly this once, in language plain
enough so that this time, for once
there'll be no mistakes. It *wants*
it says, do you understand, *wants*,
says it so plainly that you wince,
look at your feet. O dear sweet dog,
big, wet tongue hanging out, dogged,
chasing its fast cars, its busses,
fast clouds, who, despite all, busses
you with its bright dog kisses, loves
you, wags its tail back and forth, laves
its doggy self on your bowed head.
And you whisper, at last, let's head
home, and it understands, *yes, si,
oui, watch out for cars, have mercy.*

Acknowledgments

I would like to thank the editors of the following magazines in which these poems first appeared:

Agni: "The Wide World";

Apalachee Review: "Rocking Chairs from the Thirties";

Blink: "After the Argument";

Carolina Quarterly: "Beholden: On the Birth of My Daughter," "Cleave," "With Child" (published as "For My Wife, Pregnant");

The Drunken Boat (www.thedrunkenboat.com): "Baby Daughter Half Asleep in a Swing," "Mapless World," "The Neglected Moon" (published as "Baudelaire's Moon,") "Our Home Movies," "This Kingdom";

The Formalist: "The Poet at Seven";

The Georgia Review: "Digging";

The New Republic: "Mint of the Empire," "The Poet," "Signs and Portents";

The New Criterion: "One Wind";

The Paris Review: "Autobiography: The Early Years," "The World Before Them";

Ploughshares: "A Boy and His Dog";

Poetry: "Brief Monologue of the Mirror," "Homesickness" (published as "Du Bellay's Homesickness,") "London, 1943," "On Turning Fifty," "The World's Deserts";

Quarterly West: "Marianne Moore Late at Night";

Sewanee Theological Review: "Arguing About Moving to a Larger Home— What I Should Have Said," "Dreaming of Mexico, Ambrose Bierce, and Weldon Kees," "The Hippopotamus at the Zoological Gardens, Regent's Park, 1852," "Pantoum: Polish Farmhouse, 4 AM, 1943," "River," "Sparrow Falling";

Shenandoah: "The Coroner's Report";

The Southern Review: "Flowers, Things Vital and Unvital," "The Last Evening";

The Virginia Quarterly Review: "In the Hangar of Brisbee, Oklahoma, 1933."

"Baby Daughter Half Asleep in a Swing" was awarded the Cecil Hemley Memorial Award from the Poetry Society of America.

"Cleave" was reprinted on *Poetry Daily* (www.poems.com).

I am most grateful for the individual feedback I received on the poems. In particular, I would like to thank John Balaban, Al Benthall, Michael Gorelick, Don Justice, Ivonne Lamazares, Campbell McGrath, Elena Perez, Rebecca Seiferle, and Peter Schmitt. I am also indebted to the Sewanee Writers' Conference and to the Bread Loaf Writers' Conference for fellowships. Many thanks to Teresa Smith for her translation of "Homesickness" from the French, and Sigrid Rath for "The Last Evening" from the German. The Florida Arts Council has been most generous in its continued support. And my heartfelt thanks to Mitchell Kaplan for his relentless support of writers.

And also, much appreciation for Thom Ward, Peter Conners, and Susie Cohen at BOA for their care and dedication.

About the Author

Steve Kronen is the author of a previous book of poems, *Empirical Evidence* (University of Georgia Press, 1992). His poems have appeared in *Poetry, The New Republic, The Georgia Review, The Paris Review, The Threepenny Review, The American Scholar, The Drunken Boat,* and other magazines. He is the recipient of fellowships from the Bread Loaf Writers' Conference and the Sewanee Writers' Conference, two grants from the Florida Arts Council, and the Cecil Hemley Memorial Award from the Poetry Society of America. He is a librarian in Winter Park, Florida, where he lives with his wife, novelist Ivonne Lamazares, and their daughter, Sophie.

BOA Editions, Ltd.
American Poets Continuum Series

Colophon

Splendor, poems by Steve Kronen, was set in Garamond with Bodoni ormanents by Richard Foerster. The cover design was by Steve Smock. The cover art, "Crystal," by Robert Marx, is courtesy of the artist. Manufacturing by McNaughton & Gunn, Lithographers, Saline Michigan.

The publication of this book was made possible, in part, by the special support of the following individuals:

Alan & Nancy Cameros
Gwen & Gary Conners
Burch & Louise Craig
Susan DeWitt Davie
Peter & Suzanne Durant
Bev & Pete French
Dane & Judy Gordon
Kip & Deb Hale
Peter & Robin Hursh
Robert & Willy Hursh
Louise H. Klinke
Archie & Pat Kutz
Rosemary & Lew Lloyd
Jerrold & Barbara Mink
Jimmy & Wendy Mnookin
Boo Poulin
Robert H. Smith
Pat & Michael Wilder